$\mathcal{M}$ANGER
in the
MOUNTAINS

James Arne Nestingen

Augsburg
MINNEAPOLIS

MANGER IN THE MOUNTAINS

Illustrated by Barbara Knutson
Cover design by David Meyer
Text design by James Satter

ISBN 0-8066-4030-8

Manufactured in the U.S.A.   AF 9-4030

03   02   01   00   2   3   4   5   6   7   8   9   10

Foreword

I F JESUS WERE BORN TODAY, WHO WOULD COME TO THE manger? What hearts would hear the angels sing? Where would humble minds glimpse God? Where might today's Bethlehem be?

These story devotions are a daily journey from your home to humble places like the village where Christ was born. Each day in December you are invited to meet people who gather at the manger with us, even though they are far away. In them we will see the gospel drama of love and hope unfold as it did in Jesus' day. And in Advent, as we wait with the whole world for the coming child, we are especially moved by just these kinds of stories of faith in that baby who is Lord of all.

Leading us toward Bethlehem is James Arne Nestingen, storyteller and professor. Peru and Bolivia are another kind of Judea, where he sees firsthand the work he and his family have so long supported through Lutheran World Relief. His gift is to tell the story of the work and the people. Barbara Knutson, a world artist with an eye for God's creation, brings the stories to life on the page. Final thanks goes to LWR's Latin America director Jeff Whisenant, and Andean regional staff members Pedro Veliz and Jaime Bravo.

Through their stories, follow the people in these pages to the manger. With them, meet Jesus this Advent, and we will all, no matter where we live, sing Christmas praises together.

JONATHAN FRERICHS
Lutheran World Relief

Preface

QUILTS DO WONDERS, PROVIDING WARMTH AND A NIGHT'S sleep for people under the most difficult conditions. Lutheran World Relief has provided such miracles by the carload, the shipload, and the truckload all over the globe. In the process, LWR has developed a whole range of human services, becoming one of the most effective organizations in the whole world for working with people in the midst of trouble.

"Relief" is an old word from another time that smells of soup kitchens and bank checks to tide people over. LWR knows something better: the power of partnership, the joy of mutual respect, and shared humanity. So when there is trouble anywhere, people start asking for LWR.

Our family got involved with LWR when our three sons were small. Carolyn Storaasli Nestingen, my wife, and I started sending some of our family's yearly donation directly to the LWR offices. June Braun, in charge of special gifts, was nice enough to send us letters describing projects that we were supporting in our small way. We read those letters around the family table in the evening, using them as part of our devotions. Our boys, grown now and independent, still remember June's letters, as do we, with thanks.

Finally, after years of love for LWR, Carolyn and I got the chance to go and see some of the work firsthand. In arrangements generously made by Jonathan Frerichs, we traveled to Peru and Bolivia with Lita Johnson, who directs the world hunger appeal for the Evangelical Lutheran Church in America, and with Jeff Whisenant, who has been in charge of LWR's efforts in Latin America. Traveling for two weeks in December, during the Advent season, we met some others there who hosted us—Martin Blum, Pedro Veliz, and Jaime Bravo—great people who, like Jeff and Lita, won from us deep affection and admiration.

In our kitchen during December, as the days grow short and dark, hangs an old Advent calendar. Tattered, the felt a little thumb-worn, it has twenty-five pictures covered with felt pieces that can be snapped off to reveal another figure from the Christmas story. There's no mystery left in the calendar—we have used it so long, each member of the family knows what's under each cover. But it still carries us toward the mysteries and the joys of Christmas.

In a similar way, these devotions will serve you, and whoever of yours is still at your table, in your Advent journey. This year you are joined by great company, the magnificent people of Peru and Bolivia who work with and cherish the work of LWR. Hopefully, you can hear them say through all of this, "We'll meet you at the manger, and we'll meet you again, too, when many come from east and west—and north and south—to eat bread with Christ Jesus in the coming kingdom." Our family joins them in the greeting: a joyous Advent to you, and when the time comes, Merry Christmas.

JAMES ARNE NESTINGEN

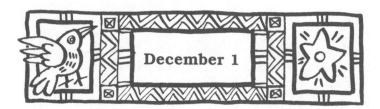

I T IS TIME TO START TOWARD THE MANGER. IT IS TIME to prepare again for Christ's coming. It is Advent and we begin in the wilderness. Have you ever been there? Maybe you have, deep in the woods, perhaps, or far out in a desert. Or maybe you just got lost on a strange street or were separated from your people in a store. Wilderness is about being lost, where the way home is not at all clear.

The countries of Peru and Bolivia, on the Pacific shoulder of South America, aren't wilderness to the people who live there. From the deserts along the Peruvian coast, to the highlands that rise green and lush between the deserts and the mountains, to the high Andes—the great mountains of both countries—or to the Amazon basin, both Peruvians and Bolivians know this land as home, as familiar to them as your yard is to you.

But to a group of us who traveled the Andes during one Advent season, it all seemed new and strange—not quite as wild as wilderness, but surely not home either. We went to learn how people in this part of the world prepare for Christ's coming. We also went to see the work of Lutheran World Relief, an organization that serves people who are caught in other kinds of wilderness—who are trying to find their way out of disaster, to shelter, some safety, or a job. As we traveled, we met all kinds of people on their way to the manger, and we found the Christ child, born again, in our day.

✧ *Find Peru and Bolivia on a map. How would you get there if you were going to go?*

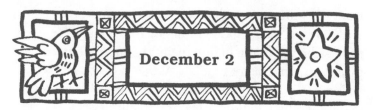

SOMETIMES, EVEN HOME CAN BECOME A WILDERNESS. As well as you know your way around, as safe as it has always been, all of a sudden everything changes, nothing is the same, and you can feel lost even in your own bed.

Off the coast of Peru, every so often the sun and moon play a strange trick on the ocean and an immense patch of ocean water starts to warm up. When this happens, it makes such a big difference that the weather changes around the world. Tornadoes break loose, there are huge rainstorms in some places and no rain at all in others, there are floods and droughts—people lose their way. Their homes turn wild.

Other things can also turn people's homes into a wilderness. If a father or mother loses a job or can't find work, food can disappear from the table. There might not be a home to live in. Sometimes governments go bad. Instead of keeping the peace and arranging things so that they are fair and just, leaders sometimes use their power to get their own way no matter what it does to other people. Then there really isn't a home.

Then the security we count on is no longer, and everything is a mess.

The people of Peru and Bolivia know that these different kinds of wildernesses can take their homes away. Strong and full of faith, they know the help that comes from a different *el niño*—the child in the manger. No matter what or where, he is at home—especially in the wilderness, with people who are lost.

✧ *What would it be like to lose your home? Who would you rely on?*

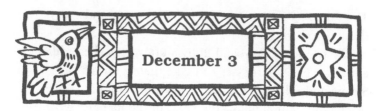

December 3

THEY COULD EACH REMEMBER THE NIGHT THAT IT happened, as though it were just one or two before. And when they told of it, they fought with tears. Trying to find their way out of the wilderness, the wilderness had found them all over again, taking away what little they had.

The people lived outside of Chiclayo *(CHICK-lai-o)*, a town on the Northern coast of Peru. Originally from the highlands, up on the edge of the mountains, they had been forced to migrate. Bad weather, a lack of jobs, and rebels fighting the government had forced them to move.

So, when the wilderness took away their homes, these people—hundreds of them—set up in the desert outside of Chiclayo. There they built a village of houses with dirt floors and walls made out of woven straw mats. They were just beginning to make a go of it when *El Niño's* rains broke lose, right in the desert. That night, the terrible one, even these homes were washed away.

But the real *El Niño*, the baby in the Christmas manger, had a different idea. He sent people who have helped work in soup kitchens, build better roofs, and improve living conditions. It's just like Jesus. When he goes to work, even a desert village can feel like home. After all, he had to migrate himself a time or two (Matthew 2:16-23).

✦ *What is a soup kitchen?*

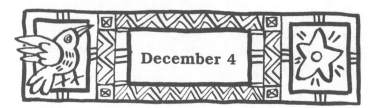

December 4

BANKS ARE USUALLY RIGHT IN THE CENTER OF THINGS, and most bankers look like they are better with money than they are with pigs or chickens. But some bankers have a different look about them.

In Sialupe (*see-ah-LOU-pay*), the bank was in a farm kitchen. The bankers weren't wearing suits; they were all dressed for other kinds of work—picking eggs, working in the fields, or selling items at the market. Besides such work, the bankers also were wives and mothers who had lots to do at home.

When there isn't enough money to make a home, women and children get hurt the worst. The menfolk, husband or sons, are forced to take work where they can find it, usually some place beyond the village—in fields, in mines, or maybe in factories. The women stay behind, tending home and children, trying to make do.

Because of this, Lutheran World Relief starts "piggy banks," small funding banks that need only a room in which to meet. Each banker begins with a loan to start a small business. They qualify for bigger loans by repaying the first. The bankers benefit twice: they have money to make a better home, and they have the joy of some independence. Maybe one of the bankers will sell you a cold drink so that you don't get thirsty going toward the manger. She will tell you, too, about all the help the Christ child gives—freely.

✧ *How might you use a dollar to help another person?*

December 5

ONE MORNING ABOVE CAJAMARACA *(ka-ha-MAR-ka)*, a beautiful town in the Peruvian Andes, we met an old man who had been a serf. He had worked on one of the *haciendas (ah-si-EN-das)*, a huge ranch, until he was freed. He wore his years in his eyes. Now he watched with a soft smile as his son shared new hopes.

Being a serf is a wilderness of its own: you never have a home of your own. Instead, like a slave, you are owned by a big landowner. He tells you when and where to work and pays you as little as possible, maybe a quarter a week, but he lets you keep most of what you grow in your garden. Maybe, just maybe, on Christmas Eve he'll let you sing Christmas carols to him and to his family.

This is a tough way to live. And things didn't get much better when their government tried to help. They broke up the big ranches, the haciendas, and freed the serfs. But the land left for the serfs was poor and they didn't have much.

A local agency started an irrigation project. With water, instead of getting only one crop a year, the children of the old serf were getting three. After years of getting buy on little or nothing, they finally had some money—enough to make a home in what had been a wilderness for them. So as the old man listened happily, his son talked irrigation and the Christ child—a future of hope.

✧ *If you don't water a plant, will it still grow?*

ONE NIGHT BEFORE CHURCH, SOUTH OF LIMA, PERU, we met with a woman who told us about another kind of wilderness. Like the people in Chiclayo, she and her family had been forced out of the highlands. But this time it wasn't because of the weather or a money shortage, but rebels.

Sometimes, when people think that the government is doing wrong and won't improve, they try to force a change. They become rebels or revolutionaries, and sometimes they use guns and other weapons to fight the government.

But the woman who came to talk with us told about a different side to revolutions. She had just come from work, wearing a T-shirt with the name of a multinational company on it. At first, she told us about how hard it had been to migrate, to leave her hometown and her family and all the others to start all over again.

Then, very carefully, the woman—who was president of her congregation—told us why she had left. The rebels had taken over their area, forcing their sons to join them and killing everyone who stood in the way. Her hometown had become a wilderness where no one was safe, not even at home.

But she knew the way to the manger, and so did the other people in church that night. We listened together as the pastor told of the Christ child, who makes a home for all of us. We're all welcome and safe at the manger.

✦ *Ask an adult to tell you the story of when he or she left home.*

J UST OUT OF LA PAZ, BOLIVIA, IS A LARGE PRISON— the high walls are brown and scary, even in the bright sun. As we passed it, the man driving told us that the families of prisoners are required to provide them with food while they're in jail.

Later on, we found out how the man knew such a detail: his wife had been in that prison. They had gotten married when they were both students at the university. Government officials suspected that they sympathized with the rebels and arrested her. While she was in prison, their first child was born.

Soon afterward their luck seemed to change. The government offered to release the woman if she and her husband promised to take their child and go into exile. Like Mary, Joseph, and Jesus—who escaped from Herod the king by going to Egypt—this Bolivian family fled to Sweden, where they made a new life for themselves.

Living in a foreign country isn't that easy. So when the government changed in Bolivia, the husband wanted to go back, the wife wanted to stay in Sweden, and their children didn't know where home was—in Bolivia or

Sweden. Their home and their family had become a wilderness.

In Advent we talk about all kinds of wilderness. Jesus comes into every one, whether in the Andes or the U.S. Jesus comes not just to show the way. Jesus comes to bring us to the manger. There we meet everyone else. There God meets us in a little child.

✤ *Have you ever been homesick? What was it like? What did you miss the most?*

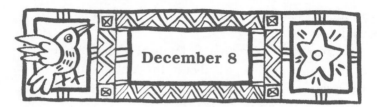

E VEN IN THE WILDERNESS, NO MATTER HOW DEEP or empty, the good Lord can always find a voice. Isaiah, the great prophet of the Old Testament who spoke for God when his people were in captivity, was a voice. John the Baptist was another. Through them, God brought home the Word—the promise of the baby in the manger who brings everyone home.

We heard the prophets' voices in the Andes. They belonged to people who had been in one kind of wilderness or another, sounding words of warning in the language of hope. They could see the hard edges, the difficult challenges, the obstacles that were making it hard, if not impossible, for their people to find their way home. Like Isaiah or John the Baptist, they have distinctive names—like Hermann or Braulio. In the next days, you'll meet them, moving toward the manger beside you.

✧ *Read the story of John the Baptist. (See Matthew 3, Mark 1:1-11, or Luke 3:1-20.)*

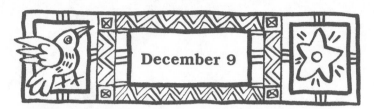

December 9

HAVE YOU EVER SEEN A PICTURE OF JOHN THE BAPTIST? He looks pretty tough, just right for a desert preacher: no shirt, a big wide camel skin around his middle, and an angry look on his face. You don't have to look like that to be like John, though; you just have to know God's promise and be willing to help people find a better way home.

We met a university professor who was a lot like John the Baptist. He was on his way to the manger, but he wasn't wearing camel's hair. His name was Hermann and he had just retired as director of a local organization called Solidarity.

Farming is hard work no matter where you live, and farmers always have a hard time getting a fair price. In Peru and Bolivia there are even more difficulties— problems with the land, using old methods, and finding markets. The Solidarity organization works with farmers helping them to find better ways.

It can be pretty discouraging. The world over, rural people are getting pushed out of a way of life that has given them a home. How can you be hopeful when you see so much trouble? "We have to be hopeful," Hermann said, "that is our duty. If we lost hope, we couldn't be of any help to our neighbors, our people."

And where do you find such hope? In the manger, in that little child laying there kicking his feet! In him, God's promise has two feet to stand on, to go to work with. In this little child is God's voice to give us a better way.

✧ *If you were John the Baptist, what would you say to our world about a better way? (See Luke 3:10-14.)*

WHEN WE WERE VISITING AT SOLIDARITY, HERMANN told us about another Isaiah or John the Baptist type. He is a farmer named Braulio, a prophet with his own radio station. The next day, we went up to see him.

Rough handed, straight talking, wearing an old black T-shirt and a pair of jeans, Braulio looked and spoke like he had just come in from doing chores. He didn't like to talk about himself very much—but as we visited, his story unfolded. Like everyone else, he had been having his share of trouble farming. But then he had heard about Solidarity and started taking some of their courses. First he learned about improved farming methods, and thereafter he never missed a course. Gradually his farm improved, and Braulio started working to help other farmers do the same.

Getting the radio station hadn't been easy. There was equipment to buy and a license to get from the government. People who owned other radio stations nearby and some other powerful people weren't so sure that they wanted Braulio broadcasting. But he went at the problems like weeds in a field, clearing them out a row at a time. As we stood with him and some of his friends, he pulled out a pocket tape recorder to interview us for a future broadcast.

Isaiah and John the Baptist were voices in the wilderness. So is Braulio, broadcasting information so people can improve their farms, make a home, and hear the voice of the Christ child, calling good news from the manger in his cry.

✦ *If Braulio were interviewing you, what kinds of questions might he ask?*

December 11

As WE CRESTED AN 11,000-FOOT RIDGE, WE LOOKED
back across a beautiful valley spreading out below
us. But when we looked over the other side we saw a big
gash, as though a gigantic knife had slashed into the
mountainside.

Our destination was Cajamarca *(ka-ha-MAR-ka),* where
five hundred years ago the Inca king surrendered to
Spanish conquerors. After twice filling a room to the top
of his outstretched hand with gold to ransom himself and
his people, the Inca king was murdered anyway. Now, in
what some have called a second conquest, a Canadian
and French company have tapped that gold again and
opened that gash. Originally intended to pay for itself in
ten years, the mine and the land have been pushed hard.
The company has its money back in less than two.

Later that afternoon, we sat with a group of pastors
and a poet talking about traveling through Advent to the
manger. The poet, a young woman whose language was
powerful and full of imagery, was another John the Baptist. The mine had ripped through her people's way of
life just as it had torn up the ground, she said. Although

her people get paid for their work, they carry the cost of the mine in very real ways: drugs and alcohol, crime, broken families. The mine's riches went away, back to Canada or France, or to the local government. "Cost recovery," she said, "is all in your perspective. Easy money is expensive."

Then she began to speak of another family, of Joseph and Mary trudging towards Bethlehem. She spoke of the child born there and of her people's Christmas songs. For prophets and poets, sadness and happiness fit right together. She could imagine hope and a future. She could see the manger.

✦ *Choose an earth trouble (like a recent environmental issue) that worries you and pray about it.*

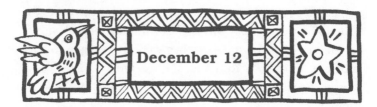

December 12

WHILE PEOPLE ALL OVER THE WORLD ARE MOVING toward the manger, preparing for Christ's coming, another church holiday interrupts Advent. Called the Immaculate Conception, it remembers the Virgin Mary. In a little town north of La Paz, Bolivia, it is just about as big as Christmas. An Isaiah or a John the Baptist shows up even here.

Looking like a sleepy town in a movie western, Laja (*LA-ha*) has two worlds in it. One includes a mix of old Incan religions with the Catholicism of the Spanish conquerors. In practices dating back centuries, people who hold this combination carry play money, dolls, model cars, and houses up the hill at the edge of town. They offer these things to a statue of the Virgin Mary for blessing, hoping that this ritual will give them what they wish for—money, a baby, a car, or a house—in the coming year.

In the afternoon, around the square, another world goes on parade, led by the village priests, who had been sent from Spain. Behind the priests another statue of the Virgin is carried. While the poorer folks went up the hill, the wealthy—many of them back in Laja for a holiday visit—and the town officials paraded with the priests.

Two Bolivian pastors watched, Isaiah and John the Baptist in disguise. They were trying to sort false hopes from real hopes, itching to shout out the hope of the manger. They wanted to tell the truth to rich and poor alike—the Christ child is the beginning of a new world for everyone.

✧ *What do we carry in our church "parades" or processions?*

December 13

J OSEPH WAS A CARPENTER. DO YOU SUPPOSE MARY
could have been one, too? Maybe if she had been a
young Aymara *(eye-MA-ra)* Indian women living above
La Paz, she would have met another John the Baptist
who could have trained her to be just that.

He had the look of a John the Baptist, tall and long-
armed with a full gray beard and flying hair. A German
man, he had been sent to Bolivia as a missionary long
enough ago to have become more at home in Bolivia
than in his homeland. He talked in a lickety-split manner
to dramatize what he was saying.

Burkhard Sievers *(SEE-verz)*, missionary and pastor,
had seen what was happening to women and their children when there was no work available. So he started a
group called Yatiyawi *(yah-tee-YAH-wee)*, designing and
building furniture out of pine and bamboo. He began
training unemployed women from the area, setting up
a carpenter's school. At the same time, he started building a factory, purchasing the machines and hand tools
needed. Within not so many years, the women were
being recognized as some of the finest carpenters in the

country, and their furniture was marketed as far away as Germany and the U.S. Soon he was not the only one speaking a word of hope.

As we walked through, we saw the women—and an occasional man—hard at work, their long black braids tied together behind them so they wouldn't drop into the blade of a table saw. These carpenter women straightened what once were crooked paths. They dared to learn, and point people to the manger, to a promise and hope.

✧ *What do you dream of doing when you grow up?*

THE CHRISTMAS STORY PUTS THEM TOGETHER SO closely that it seems like they belong in the same breath: angels and shepherds. But in Bible times, it wouldn't take a John the Baptist to tell you that these two generally don't fit—unless it's Jesus working.

Angels aren't so pious in the Bible. They have hard work to do, carrying God's messages around. And they get sent to some rough places where it would be pretty tough to keep their wings clean—Abraham and Sarah's tent, for example, or the furnace where Daniel was thrown. Still, angels are holy, going about God's work, and if one visited, you might be a little frightened.

If you met a shepherd, though, your first question would probably be different: "How long since that guy had a bath?" Shepherds usually live out in the wilderness, where the only showers are rain. Shepherds don't get much of a chance to go to church, either, being far away. In the old days most anybody would say that shepherds have to be watched.

When Jesus goes to work—even if it's just kicking and crying in a manger—holy angels and dirty shepherds get

32

together. Some ordinary people turn out to be angels, and some shepherds—dirty fingernails and all—turn out to be saints. Look around you at the manger. Who are you? Who is next to you?

✧ *Read about the angels and shepherds in Luke 2:8-20.*

ANGELS USUALLY HAVE SOME ALTITUDE—THEY COME
down from heaven, as the Bible says—so you might
not expect to see one in a black derby hat, especially
with the brim turned down. There she was, though,
coming out of a greenhouse at 14,500 feet, her arms full
of vegetables. Around the corner she even had a pig.
And, off at work somewhere, a husband.

Okay, going by the stories of Michael the archangel
and all of the others, the tomatoes, that hog, and the kids
hiding behind her skirt might disqualify Valentina as an
angel. Yet angels are full of surprises (aren't they?) and
sometimes they have to get their aprons dirty, especially
if they start hanging around mangers and stables.

Valentina, the angel, has a house full of kids—and
with her husband has a tough time feeding them. Clouds
do a better job of growing hail and frost then they do
crops. The family has had meat, either pork or llama,
but living so high up, not a very balanced diet.

That was until Valentina heard about the greenhouse
project worked out by Lutheran World Relief and one of
its partner agencies. With short adobe walls, a big spread

of heavy plastic and the intense, high altitude sun, the temperature inside runs about 120 degrees in the afternoon and a garden grows—tomatoes, potatoes, lettuce, cabbage, and maybe even some good red beets. "And do you know what's happened since I built my greenhouse?" the angel asked. "My kids' grades have improved."

Look around the manger—what "foods" are angels leaving you?

✧ *Make a list of all the food you've had today. Is your diet balanced?*

THE MAN PICKED UP A SMOOTH STONE AND PUT IT IN a sling, much like the one David used against some lions in Bible times. For David it was two long strings with a pocket tied between them. This one was all one piece, made of alpaca wool. The man whirled the sling behind his back and over his head a couple of times, one string dropped and the rock flew, fast and straight and far. He had killed foxes with that sling when they bothered the sheep.

The man lives high in a mountain valley under a spreading sky that is such a dark blue that it's almost purple. He is a shepherd, like David was before he was king. He is a shepherd, like the ones who came to the manger.

He whistled and the llamas lined up as though it were time for lunch. The sheep spread out behind them. Funny looking, like camels with their humps cut off, the llamas stood looking at him, chewing their cud, wondering what would come next.

Jesus must have learned to whistle, too, when he got older. But in that manger, he squalled instead, calling us to come and be there with him. Maybe if you're lucky, that old mountain shepherd will be the one standing next you, sling hanging out of his back pocket—though you won't have to worry about foxes or lions. As the prophet Isaiah saw it, they'll be playing with the lambs, and maybe even a few young llamas. At the manger, they'll want you to play, too.

✧ *Read Isaiah 11:6-9 and draw a picture of how God imagines the world could be.*

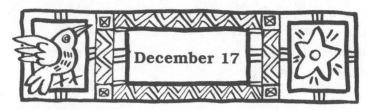

December 17

W HAT WOULD YOU THINK IF YOU MET AN ANGEL who had thinning black hair, was short, and had a belly bouncing over the top of his belt? We met one in Bolivia.

Well, maybe he isn't really an angel but he sure has the touch of one. His name is pronounced *HAI-may* in Spanish, but it's spelled like "Jaime." His mother was an Aymara Indian from La Paz, the mountain city two miles high in the Andes. His father worked for the electrical company. As a young man, Jaime became a Methodist pastor. He carried God's message to his people, just like angels are supposed to do, telling them of Christ Jesus.

But Jaime wanted to see God's message at work, too. So he began to study ways to work with people who don't usually get much of a chance at making a living—mountain farmers or shepherds, for example, or miners who have been put out of work, or farm women unable to get the money to go to market. Now when Jaime goes to work, he always has a joke, a laugh, a pat on the back, an arm over the shoulder, some encouragement, a word of hope, a gift to give in Christ, or a song to sing. You don't have to look like an angel or sing from the clouds to God's messenger—all you need is God's words, some good hands, and a heart about the size of Jaime's. The Christ child will give you one, as he did Jaime.

✧ *Look at the list of what Jaime does as he works. Pick one and do it with someone today.*

A S THE CHRISTMAS STORY USUALLY GETS TOLD, THERE are cows, sheep, and at least one donkey around the baby Jesus, but don't you think there should be some chickens, too? They don't just cluck and lay eggs. They can even pay the bills.

Near the area where the Andes tumble down into the Amazon, where this mighty river of South America—one of the greatest rivers of the whole world—flows toward the Atlantic Ocean, there are some women who learned how to make chickens work for them. These women had lots of responsibilities in their families and their communities, but not much of a chance to make money. Their husbands usually didn't earn much; it was tough for everyone, especially the children.

But someone had an idea, one that lots of farm people remember: "egg money." This is money on the side, the little bit of extra cash earned by selling eggs. And chickens make good soup, especially if you've got a cold. And they'll make a wonderful Sunday dinner, too. In fact, people will pay hard cash for eggs and even more for the whole chicken.

So the women start raising chickens, a few here, a few there, as many as each of them could. Pretty soon they had eggs to sell, enough to supply the whole town. And it wasn't long before they had enough chickens to start selling them at the market. There'll be some chickens at the manger, alright, and with them some women giving thanks to Jesus for their chickens and a whole new way of life.

✦ *How does your family earn money?*

ANOTHER WORD FOR "SHEPHERD" IS "PASTOR." MAYBE that's not such good news. If you have a pastor, you're a sheep. But there is something wonderful about it, too. A pastor speaks God's word and stands with people when they are in trouble, just like a shepherd, fighting off foxes or lions. In Bolivia, many of the pastors have an additional name—they are called "barefoot." They all wear shoes, at least now, but most of them work without any pay, relying on other jobs and what other help they can find to serve their people. Like their people, they have little money.

One night in La Paz, we met with about thirty of the "barefoot" pastors to talk about getting ready for Christmas. One by one, they told of how difficult it has been. As hard as they work, their people barely provide for themselves and their families; there is little freedom; the parents could only dream about a time when they could give their children Christmas presents. One pastor said he was embarrassed because he had two shirts while his parishioners have only one apiece. Unlike them, he has a shirt to wear on wash days.

The pastors were asked, "What gives you hope?" The two-shirted, barefoot pastor stood quietly. "My name is Castro," he said. "I serve Jesus Christ, who loves us sinners and raises the dead." Pastor Castro will be beside the manger with you, giving thanks for the promise of Christ Jesus.

✧ *Walk barefoot for a time today to feel what it's like to be too poor for shoes.*

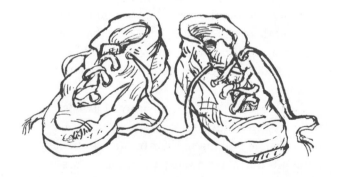

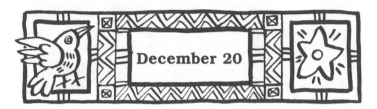

WHAT IF AN ANGEL WANTED TO WASH YOUR HANDS? You don't need any help, you say? But what if washing them properly could save your life? Then it wouldn't be so bad to have an angel, or someone like one, leaning over your shoulder—taking your hands— to show you how.

Dirty water can be as dangerous as clean water is good, especially when the dirty water breaks loose in torrents. This happened in Peru during the last big *El Niño,* when the rains sent floods down the mountains, picking up sewage and dead animals along with all the other debris. Cholera, a killing disease, threatened to become an epidemic, adding its toll to the other damage that had been done.

When the floods broke loose, an army of angels mobilized. They were student nurses from the university who were far enough along in their training to be helpful. Moving out into the troubled areas, the nurses-in-training volunteered their love and knowledge, besides everything else, teaching children and anyone who wanted a lesson in how to wash hands.

You start at your elbows and work toward your fingers until each one of them has been washed individually. Then, with fresh water, you start down the other arm. Jesus will be happy to take a dirty hand, but maybe one of the angels around the stable will help you with yours.

✧ *Wash your hands the way the student nurses taught.*

WITH CHRISTMAS JUST AROUND THE CORNER, MARY and Joseph are coming near. The Wise Men are coming, too. It won't be long—a couple of weeks by the church's calendar but a few days by the way the story usually is told—before the kings show up with their presents and we start opening ours.

In most of North America, Mary, Joseph, and the three kings all should be wearing jackets, and Jesus shouldn't be just wrapped in only swaddling clothes. Where's his quilt? A person could freeze lying in a manger up here.

Old Mr. Sun goes south for the winter. So while most of us northern types are skating, skiing, or hoping the oranges and grapefruit won't be damaged by a frost, the people in Peru and Bolivia enjoy Christmas as a summer holiday. No one dreams of a white Christmas. Instead, there are explosions of color, especially down the eastern slopes of the Andes into the Amazon basin, flowers big as cake tins and smelling just as sweet.

The colors show in the people, too. A mixture of Indian and Spanish ancestry makes beautiful brown skin. And the shawls and blankets are vivid purples, pinks,

reds, yellows—a real rainbow. Can you imagine them—
a whole crowd of your brothers and sisters in Christ
looking north from under a blazing sun. *"Feliz Navidad,"*
they're shouting, "Merry Christmas." But we all sing that,
in whatever language is ours. This baby we await is
coming for all of us!

✧ *What would it be like to have Christmas in the*
   summer?

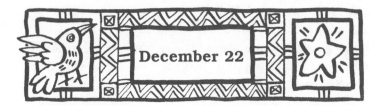

December 22

What do you suppose would have happened if one of the Wise Men had shown up early? "There's nothing here but an old stable," he might have said. "That manger looks pretty rickety." But it could have happened, yes? The Wise Men were led by a star that appeared just one time.

There are other kinds of "wise men," though, wise men and wise women who show up around the manger, children of the Christ child. Pedro is such a person, and he seems to show up at the just he right time.

Pedro's heart is bigger than he is. Born in Lima, Peru, his father was a street vendor, standing on the sidewalk, selling things to people who passed by. It's a hard way to make a living. Maybe Pedro's wisdom came from his parents; knowledge he got at the university, studying there just as Peru's old economy began to change. He has spent all of his life working with people who have gotten left out or put at the edges, helping them to use their abilities to give their gifts to the world around them.

When Pedro works with people, his big heartedness and his wisdom show. Soft-spoken, tenderly, with a constantly alert eye, he welcomes everyone, asks probing questions, offers an encouraging word, gives a blessing. You wouldn't see Pedro next to the manger—he would be off to the side checking on the donkey, making sure the shepherds get their chance, winking at an angel, smiling softly at the sound of Christ's voice. He is there, though, with all his gifts, giving at every turn.

✧ *Have you met a wise person like Pedro? Read the story of the Wise Men in Matthew 2:1-12.*

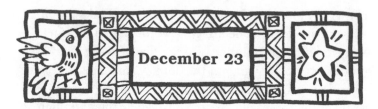

ALTHOUGH IT DOESN'T SAY SO IN THE BIBLE, WHEN those three Wise Men were ambling along on their camels, following the star, someone had to be wise enough to think about the nitty-gritty questions: How much farther do we have to go? What are we going to have for lunch? What's going to happen if these camels were watered seven days ago instead of six? The Wise Men needed this kind of person or they never would have made it to the manger.

Such a wise man led our trip to the Andes: Señor Jeff, we called him—Mister Jeff. At least we thought him wise, until one day, with a big smile playing at the corner of his lips, he ordered up a meal Andean people consider a Christmas delicacy. There it is called *cuy (COU-ie);* here, guinea pig. We ran into a delightful, but real cultural hurdle.

Jeff is at the manger, too. Though he would never tell you, Jeff's wisdom about organizations—about how to make things work and get things done—has made it possible for countless others to be at the manger, too. People from all over Central and South America—Nicaraguans,

Ecuadorians, Bolivians, and Peruvians—will be smiling with us at the new baby.

✧ *Think of three countries you would love to know more about. Find them on a map.*

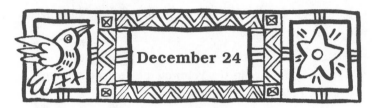

December 24

S HE SAT CROSS-LEGGED ON THE PAINTED CEMENT floor behind a small table, her young husband standing uncertainly to one side of her, other relatives arranged on either side. She was dressed like most of the women of that region: a unisex, stove-piped, straw cowboy hat with a broad brim covering her thick, black hair; a long braid disappearing behind her; a red sweater and a puffy blue skirt spread over her legs. She looked up, weeping, and then back down into her hands.

On the table lay her three-week-old son, Ivan. Under the blanket he was wrapped with a couple of layers of clothing, a sweater on top, a stocking cap pulled around his head so that the cold night air of the mountains couldn't catch him with a draft. But close as his mother's love was, it wasn't enough to spare him. Ivan, her first-born, had just died.

We had been on our way up the mountainside, four of us in the extended cab of a pickup, another four in the box, laughing, joking, and playing in the brilliant morning sunshine. We had stopped to pick up Ivan's grandaunt, who knew the family we were going to visit.

It was she, weeping, who led Pedro and me inside. Could these grieving parents be Mary and Joseph? Soon after Jesus was born, they had to fear for his death and escape to Egypt. And one day, when Jesus was grown, Mary would hold his lifeless body, weeping.

But Jesus lives. Sometimes, Easter breaks out of the calendar to take hold of Christmas, right there at the manger. Pedro said it, "Christ is risen and he will raise Ivan, too."

✧ *Remember someone you love who has died.*

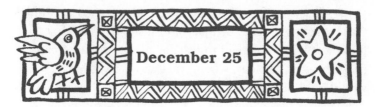

December 25

FOR ALL THE PEOPLE—AND EVEN THE ANIMALS—
that you've met at the manger, there is still one
more. He is not at it, but in it—the Christ child. You've
met him before, haven't you? But one of the wonderful
things about Jesus is that even when you know him,
you never quite do. There is always more to him.

One summery morning, we went up the side of the
bowl in which La Paz sits to visit an organization called
Yatiyawi (yah-tee-YAH-wee). Hanging across the back
wall of the shop, we saw more of Jesus. He was in a
painting called *The Christ of the Andes*. Jesus was an
Andean shepherd or farmer in that picture, towering over
the mountains below him, wearing the floppy eared
stocking cap that is a trademark of the region. Around
him are other Andean people along with some signs of
the powers that makes life difficult for them.

At Christmas, Jesus is a wee child, kicking his legs,
nuzzling Mary's breasts, burping over Joseph's shoulder.
Since the first Easter, he is the risen Lord who seeks out
his people the world over, from your house all the way
to the Andes, throughout the Americas, Asia, Africa,

Europe, and Australia. Cradled in the manger, this one is God deep in the flesh—God taking on the powers, surprising, gracing, and freeing. Above all this is God loving you in particular and the rest of us, every last one. Welcome to the manger. There's a place for you here!

✧ *Sing a Christmas song. Jesus is born!*

About the Author

JAMES ARNE NESTINGEN is Professor of Church History at Luther Theological Seminary in St. Paul, Minnesota. He is a gifted storyteller, able to integrate theology and real life, and is sought after for church gatherings across the country. His global interest goes beyond the Andes. Through the church, he has worked in Africa, at Makumira Theological College in Tanzania, and in Australia.

He is also the author of *Free to Be* (with Gerhard Forde), confirmation materials that explore Luther's Small Catechism, and *The Hidden Promise,* the 1995 Women of the ELCA Bible study, which won an Award of Merit from the Associated Church Press. James and his wife, Carolyn, live in St. Paul and have three sons.

About the Illustrator

BARBARA KNUTSON grew up in South Africa as the daughter of American missionaries. She later taught in Nigeria and lived for two years in Peru. Barbara now resides in St. Paul, Minnesota, where she illustrates picture books. Her other books include *Colors of Ghana, Hanna's Cold Winter,* and *Kwanzaa Karamu.*